I Want to Be a CROCODILE

by Thomas Kingsley Troupe

Illustrated by Christina Wald

PICTURE WINDOW BOOKS
a capstone imprint

"Kyle!" my older sister shouted. She grabbed my arm, and I totally screamed!

"Jocelyn!" I shouted. "Don't do that!"

"Ha, ha," she laughed as she left the room. "Got you!"

"I want to be a crocodile," I told the TV.
"Nobody would mess with me!"

Just like that, I turned into a crocodile. And my front yard turned into a swamp. I couldn't believe it!

Low to the ground, I moved across the grass. People nearby pointed and backed away. Would they send someone to catch me? I wasn't sure. I ran for the water.

I love to swim, but I'd never been in a swamp. The murky green water felt cool and safe. This was my home!

I swam into the swamp, heading for deeper water. I sank down until only my eyes and nostrils showed above the surface. Bugs buzzed all around. I didn't even care!

The crocs come out at night! American crocodiles like to feed at night. They spend their days resting in hidden waters or thick plants.

I relaxed and got used to my body. My snout was huge! I could see my nose at the end of it. There were almost 70 teeth inside my mouth. Wow! I would need a bigger toothbrush.

My short crocodile legs couldn't touch the bottom. Good thing I could float!

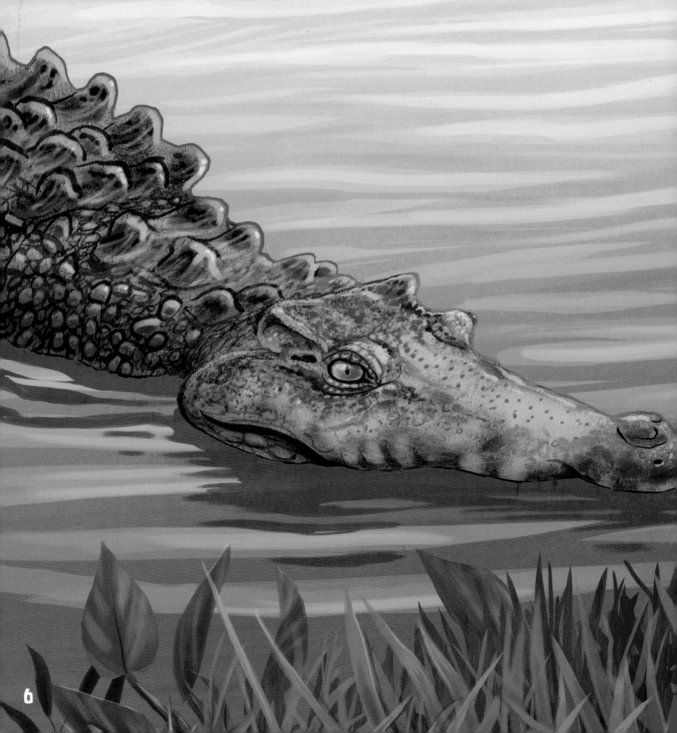

"Hey, you!" I heard a voice call. "What are you doing in my swamp?"

"Hi," I said. "I'm Kyle."

"I'm Casey," he said. "I don't usually let new crocs mess around in my space, kid. But I'll cut you a break."

We swam toward a small island. I swished my giant tail and moved quickly through the water. For a big lizard, I could really swim!

Are those crocodile tears of ... loneliness? Most crocodiles like to keep to themselves, and males are aggressive to other males.

I wanted to see what I could do with my crocodile body. I dived deep and swam around. Filmy lids covered my eyes. It was like wearing goggles in swim class! I could see all kinds of stuff below the surface.

Crocodile tails are solid muscle and help give the animals bursts of speed on land and in water.

"I should get some air," I said. It felt strange being underwater for so long.

"Why?" Casey said. "We can stay underwater for 15 minutes. Even longer if we're hiding from danger."

I thrashed my tail. I zipped through the water somewhere around 20 miles (32 kilometers) per hour! That was way faster than I could swim laps before!

For the first time ever, I wasn't afraid of anything. I rose to the surface, keeping my eyes above water. If I was still, I could look like a harmless log.

I wanted to stay in the swamp all day, just floating around!

A few crocodiles lurked on the nearby shore. One of them had his big mouth wide open.

"Is he trying to catch flies?" I asked Casey.

Casey laughed. "No, he's trying to cool off. Crocodiles sweat through their mouths."

"Yuck," I thought. "Who wants a bunch of salty sweat in his mouth?"

"Sometimes we'll roar and bellow," Casey explained. "That's a mating call."

Up ahead I saw a bird on a log. In my crocodile mind, I thought it looked tasty.

I drifted close and lunged. I opened my jaws and tried to catch the bird. SNAP! Too slow! The bird chirped and flew away into the trees.

Crocodile rock? Some crocodiles will swallow stones to help break up the food in their bellies.

"So close!" Casey said. "But don't worry, there's plenty to eat out here."

"Like what?"

"Little rodents, fish, bugs, frogs, turtles," Casey said. "Sometimes dead animals."

"Okay," I said. "I'm not so hungry anymore."

"No worries there," Casey said. "Crocodiles can go days without eating. You know, if we have to."

Some little crocodiles scrambled along the shore. An alert mama watched us from nearby.

"Why does she look so worried?" I whispered to Casey.

"Very few baby crocs survive," he said. "A lot of other creatures, including other crocodiles, will try to eat them."

Many crocodiles are eaten within their first year of life. They can be prey to big fish, hungry herons, and adult crocodiles!

"There's a crocodile eating some babies now!" I cried.

"Calm down," Casey said. "That's a mother bringing her babies to the water. She'll stay with them a bit, then leave them to survive on their own."

I watched another crocodile mama bury about 50 eggs near the swamp. She looked unhappy too. A male crocodile stood nearby, keeping his eye on us.

"Both parents will usually guard the nest, but only a few babies will hatch," Casey said. "Even crocodile eggs get eaten up by hungry animals."

"I didn't know crocodiles were in so much danger," I said.

"Little crocs can't defend themselves," Casey said. "But once they have grown, they rule the swamp."

"Often crocodiles can live to be about 70 years old,"
Casey said. "But humans are our biggest threat. They
destroy our habitat, build roads, and hunt us."

"Wow!" I shouted. "He almost got hit by a truck!"

"A lot of crocodiles end up as road kill," Casey said.
"But poachers are the worst. Our skins are worth a lot
of money. They hunt us any chance they can get."

"Makes me want to take a chomp out of them!" I said.

"Yeah," Casey said. "We don't really do that. It just causes more trouble. Plus, people taste terrible."

Casey and I slipped away so the poachers wouldn't see us.

"Great. Another shopping center," Casey said. "Don't humans have enough of those?"

COMING SOON
SUPER SHOPPER CENTER

I wondered how many nests and crocodile homes were destroyed. It made me sad, thinking of all of the crocs looking for a new place to live.

"Never mind this," Casey said. "Let's get back to the swamp while it lasts!"

"Race you there!" I shouted. As I slipped back into the tall grass ...

... I was back in my living room. Jocelyn walked by as I crawled on the floor. She didn't see me, so I grabbed her ankle.

"Gotcha!" I yelled. Jocelyn screamed like she was in a horror movie!

"Kyle!" she shouted. "Don't do that!"

"Ha-ha," I cried. "You never saw me coming!"

"No fair," Jocelyn said. "You snuck up on me. What a crock!"

"Pretty much," I said and smiled big and wide.

How can you help the crocodiles? Never buy items made from crocodile skin, for starters. You can also support wildlife conservation groups working to stop development into crocodile habitats!

Additional facts:

- A crocodile's ears have flaps that close up when its head goes underwater.

- Crocodiles have a great sense of hearing. They can hear baby crocs calling from inside their eggs.

- The crocodile's tail helps it to swim up 20 mph (32 kph). On land their tails give them short bursts of speed, making them pretty fast for creatures with such short legs.

- Crocodiles share food, but not because they like to. They work together to help eat prey they can't swallow whole.

- The temperature of a crocodile's nest affects if the baby crocs will be males or females. Nests at high and low temperatures will produce females. Temperatures in between will produce males.

Glossary

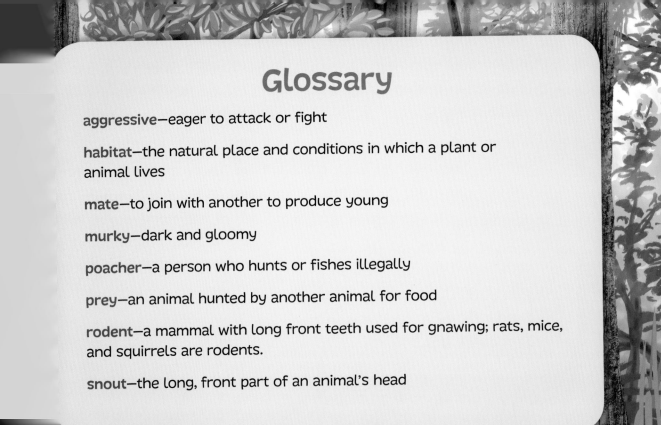

aggressive—eager to attack or fight

habitat—the natural place and conditions in which a plant or animal lives

mate—to join with another to produce young

murky—dark and gloomy

poacher—a person who hunts or fishes illegally

prey—an animal hunted by another animal for food

rodent—a mammal with long front teeth used for gnawing; rats, mice, and squirrels are rodents.

snout—the long, front part of an animal's head

Read More

Barr, Brady. *Crocodile Encounters.* Washington, D.C. National Geographic Kids Books, 2012.

Bodden, Valerie. *Amazing Animals: Crocodiles.* Mankato, Minn. Creative Education, 2010.

Thomas, Isabel. *Remarkable Reptiles.* Mankato, Minn. Heinemann Raintree, 2013.

FactHound

FactHound offers a safe, fun way to find internet sites related to this book. All of the sites on FactHound have been researched by our staff.

Here's all you do:
Visit *www.facthound.com*
Type in this code: 9781479568574

Super-cool stuff!

Check out projects, games and lots more at
www.capstonekids.com

Index

babies, 14, 15

eggs, 15, 21

eyes, 5, 8, 10, 15

habitat, 16, 20

lifespan, 16

mating, 11

poachers, 16, 17

prey, 13, 14, 21

snout, 6

swamp, 4, 5, 7, 10, 15, 18

swimming, 5, 7, 8, 9, 21

tail, 7, 8, 9, 21

teeth, 6

Books in the Series

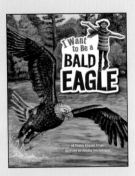
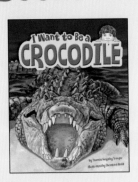

Thanks to our advisers for their expertise, research, and advice:
Michelle D. Boone, PhD
Associate Professor, Department of Biology
Miami University, Oxford, Ohio

Editors: Shelly Lyons and Nick Healy
Designer: Sarah Bennett
Creative Director: Nathan Gassman
Production Specialist: Tori Abraham

The illustrations in this book were created using acrylic paints and digital effects.
Photograph on pages 20-21: Shutterstock/Oleksandr Lysenko

Picture Window Books are published by Capstone,
1710 Roe Crest Drive, North Mankato, Minnesota 56003
www.capstonepub.com

Library of Congress Cataloging-in-Publication Data
Troupe, Thomas Kingsley, author.
  I want to be a crocodile / by Thomas Kingsley Troupe ; illustrated by Christina Wald.
      pages cm. — (Nonfiction picture books. I want to be....)
  Summary: "Text written from the animal's perspective helps teach kids about life as a crocodile"— Provided by publisher.
  Audience: Ages 5-8.
  Audience: K to grade 3.
  Includes bibliographical references and index.
  ISBN 978-1-4795-6857-4 (library binding) —
ISBN 978-1-4795-6861-1 (ebook pdf)
  1. Crocodiles—Juvenile literature. I. Wald, Christina, illustrator. II. Title.
  QL666.C925T76 2016
  597.98'2—dc23
                                                2015010234

Printed in the United States of America in Brainerd, Minnesota.
032015   008826BANGF15